LEGO

DC COMICS
SUPER HEROES

BATMAN'S MISSIONS

Written by Beth Davies

Editorial Assistant Beth Davies
Senior Editor Hannah Dolan
Designer Thelma-Jane Robb
Jacket Designer David McDonald
Senior Designer Nathan Martin
Pre-Production Producer Marc Staples
Producer Louise Daly
Managing Editors Elizabeth Dowsett, Simon Hugo
Design Manager Ron Stobbart
Art Director Lisa Lanzarini
Publisher Julie Ferris
Publishing Director Simon Beecroft

Reading Consultant
Linda B. Gambrell, Ph.D.

First American edition, 2015
Published in the United States by DK Publishing
1450 Broadway, Suite 801, New York, New York 10018
DK, a Division of Penguin Random House LLC

Page design copyright © 2020 Dorling Kindersley Limited

21 22 14 13 12 11
010-185650-Feb/2015

For the curious

www.dk.com
www.LEGO.com

Contents

Gotham City's Hero

Gotham City is a dark and dangerous place. The streets are filled with criminals and villains who want to cause trouble. The Gotham City Police Department struggles to keep them all under control. Luckily, the police have Batman to help them protect the city.

Batman wears a mask to hide his other identity—an important businessman named Bruce Wayne. Bruce loves Gotham City and vows to protect its citizens from crime. He does not have any superpowers, but he has trained very hard to increase his strength and become Batman. He has also built many tools to help him in his daring missions. Batman is the World's Greatest Detective.

Daily Training Log

Name: Batman
Day: 473

Daily Goal: My goal is to be just as awesome as I was yesterday.

ACTIVITY	TIME	NOTES	
Running	6 AM	I was awake all night fighting crime, but still went for a run this morning. I ran up a muddy hill—backward.	✔
Upside-down Meditation	8 AM	I meditated while hanging from the ceiling, but was ready to leap into action if needed.	✔
Resting	1 PM	I had a little nap, with one eye open. Crime never sleeps.	✔
Strength Training	3 PM	I spent the afternoon stretching, practicing my martial arts, and lifting weights—all at once.	✔
Refueling	4 PM	I ate a small, healthy snack to boost my energy levels. A bat eats little and often.	✔

Here I am after my
12 mile run. No sweat.

I love hanging upside
down—just like a bat.

This is me in the
gym. Looking good.

Time to put my day's
training into practice.

Robin

This is Robin, Batman's trusted sidekick and friend. He is very quick and agile. Batman is training Robin to be a great crime fighter, just like him. The brave duo have worked together on many difficult missions.

Batman has been teaching Robin
martial arts, including stick-fighting.
Robin uses his long stick to battle
Batman's enemy, the Penguin.
The Penguin's umbrella is no match
for Robin's whirling stick!

Meet the Gordons

Barbara Gordon works as a librarian during the day, but she transforms into an ace crime fighter named Batgirl at night. Batgirl battles bad guys alongside Batman and Robin. She is both brave and intelligent. Her mask and Batsuit are similar to Batman's.

Commissioner James Gordon
is the chief police officer in Gotham
City. He is Barbara's father, but he
does not know she is secretly Batgirl.
Commissioner Gordon often calls on
Batman, Robin, and Batgirl in times
of need. He shines a
bright Bat-Signal
into the night sky
when he needs
their help.

The Joker

The Joker is a crazy criminal who loves to cause chaos in Gotham City. The Joker has a big smile, but he is not friendly. This colorful villain has many scary tricks up his purple sleeves.

The Joker often uses henchmen to carry out his plans. His horrible helper wears bright clown makeup to look like his boss.

The Joker is Batman's worst enemy. Batman has defeated the Joker many times. The Joker is now locked up in Arkham Asylum. He has to wear a bright orange prison uniform, which he thinks goes wonderfully with his bright green hair!

Criminal Profile
Gotham City Police Department

NAME: *The Joker*

ALIAS: *The Clown Prince of Crime*

APPEARANCE: *He looks like a clown, with brightly colored hair and a painted face. He often wears a purple suit and always wears a giant grin.*

PROFILE: *The Joker is an insane and evil criminal. He believes all of his crimes are funny jokes.*

WEAPONS: *He has invented a powerful toxic gas.*

LOCATION: *Batman defeated the Joker's last scheme and captured him. The Joker is currently imprisoned in Arkham Asylum, and is no longer a threat to the public.*

40 mm

35 mm

30 mm

Suspect ID No. SH061-10937

SCARECROW

THE JOKER

ALERT!

Arkham Asylum

Arkham Asylum is a dark and spooky building on the edge of Gotham City. The Joker is locked up in Arkham Asylum as punishment for all the crimes he has committed. However, the Joker is not planning to stick around for long! He is plotting to break out of his cell in the middle of the night. Lots of other crazy criminals live in the cells of Arkham Asylum, too. Gotham City will be in big trouble if they are all plotting their escape.

Top-secret Escape Plan

The Joker thinks it's no joke being stuck in this silly asylum! He's been plotting his escape for weeks. His secret notes have been found stuck to the walls in his cell.

1. I'll tell the guard a joke, and when he is rolling around with laughter, I'll escape from my cell.

HH I

2. If I free the other criminals, it will make it harder for the guard to stop me!

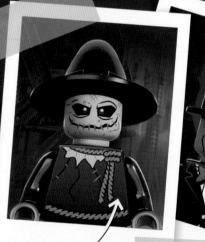

3. Next, I will jump in the security van to make my giggling getaway.

4. Finally, I will be free and the joke will be on Gotham City!

THE JOKER WAS HERE

Arkham Escape

It is a normal night at Arkham Asylum. There is only one guard on duty, who watches over the inmates and patrols the building. When the guard checks on the Joker, the Joker tells him a hilarious joke. While the guard cries with laughter, the Joker slips past him and escapes!

Look out! The Joker has released Scarecrow from his cell. Scarecrow had been put in Arkham Asylum as punishment for using a dangerous gas that gives people bad dreams. This villain's escape is Batman's worst nightmare!

Suiting Up

Bruce Wayne leaps into action when he hears about the trouble at Arkham Asylum. He must become Batman to save the day. Bruce rushes to prepare, but which Batsuit is right for the job?

This Batsuit has lots of strong armor. It is great for fighting super-strong enemies, but it is a little heavy.

Batman is hard to spot in this Arctic Batsuit, but only if he is on a mission somewhere snowy!

This Batsuit comes with a Bat-glider. It is useful if Batman needs to fly somewhere fast or track multiple enemies. Perfect!

Villains on the Loose

Batman soars into the night sky wearing his Bat-glider. It is perfect for this mission. He can see all of Arkham Asylum. The villains are escaping in different directions! Robin rushes to battle Scarecrow and the Penguin on the ground. He battles them both using his amazing martial arts skills.

The Joker is too quick for the guard, but not for Batman! Batman swoops down from above to stop the Joker in his tracks! Batman and Robin capture the villains and Gotham City is safe once more. Good work!

GOTHAM CITY

Gotham City faces new foe

Bane wears an unusual mask at all times.

GAZETTE

A criminal known only as Bane is at large in Gotham City tonight. Witnesses have reported seeing him stealing and causing terrible damage to the streets of the city.

Police Commissioner Gordon urged people to remain vigilant but calm as the police work tirelessly to capture the villain. He also warned the public not to approach Bane. He is extremely strong and is known to be violent.

Only days ago, Batman prevented an escape attempt by a group of inmates at Arkham Asylum. Tonight, the police department have lit the Bat-Signal to call for Batman's help in capturing this new threat to the city.

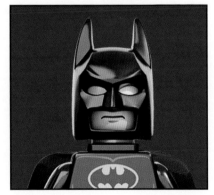

Our city's brave protector, the mysterious Batman.

Bane

Batman does not have time to rest after his battle at Arkham Asylum! Another dangerous criminal is on the loose and only Batman can stop him. Bane is known for his huge muscles and incredible strength, but he also has a clever and devious mind.

Bane's Tumbler car is tough and powerful. He uses it to race and smash through the streets of Gotham City. The vehicle has strong metal armor that protects Bane even if the car flips upside down.

On the Move

Batman has many vehicles that help him fight crime. All of them are built in his favorite color: black! His favorite car is called the Batmobile. Batman drives the Batmobile at top speeds to reach crime scenes around the city.

On some of his missions,
Batman needs to take
to the sky. His Batwing is
perfect for these jobs. Batman's
plane has two powerful jet
engines to help it speed through
the sky. Batman can also move
its huge wings forward and trap
his enemies between them.

Batman's Vehicles

Batman has designed and built a whole fleet of special vehicles, all named after himself. Each one has its own unique uses. Batman is ready for anything in these brilliant rides!

Batmobile

Use Road chases
Best features
The Batmobile is low to the ground and has large, powerful wheels. This makes it an extremely fast vehicle.

Batcopter

Use Air attacks
Best features
Powerful rotors on the Batcopter allow it to speed through the skies. It can also fire missiles to blast Batman's enemies.

Batboat

Use Ocean missions

Best features

The Batboat races across the waves with ease, thanks to the sharp blades on its side fins and a large rudder at the back.

Batsub

Use Underwater adventures

Best feature

The Batsub can travel down to the darkest depths of the ocean. It even glows in the dark to help Batman find his way.

Bat-Mech

Use Ground battles

Best features

Batman's Bat-Mech gives him extra height and strength. He can launch missiles and shoot nets at his enemies.

Batman vs. Bane

Take cover! Batman pilots a huge
flying machine called The Bat as
he chases Bane across Gotham City.
This mighty machine has two
powerful engines that propel it
through the air. It is also loaded
with dangerous missiles and Batman
is not afraid to use them!

Commissioner Gordon is tracking
Bane on the ground. Batman must
be careful not to hit his friend by
mistake. Batman takes aim and fires!
Bane's Tumbler screeches to a halt.
When Bane leaps from the car,
Commissioner Gordon
arrests him.

Crime-fighting Partners

Batman is always busy fighting crime in Gotham City. Every time he defeats a villain, another one appears with an even more evil scheme! Batman is sometimes called upon to help his fellow Super Heroes fight enemies around the world, too.

When Batman has to leave Gotham City, he asks Batgirl and Commissioner Gordon to watch over the city. He knows they won't let him—or Gotham City—down. Robin often joins him on his missions.

Aquaman

One of Batman's Super Hero friends is named Aquaman. He lives deep under the sea. Aquaman is a powerful swimmer and can travel through the water at top speed. He can also breathe underwater.

Aquaman normally carries a special golden trident, but someone has stolen it!

Batman and Robin offer to use their famous detective skills to find the trident. They do not have Aquaman's underwater powers, so they need special gadgets for this mission.

Robin has a new scuba suit with large flippers to help him swim, and air tanks to help him survive underwater. His suit also has handy blue goggles.

Black Manta

Ah ha! It's the evil Black Manta who
has stolen Aquaman's trident and now
he has captured Robin, too!

Robin does not like the robot shark
Black Manta is using to guard his lair.
The shark's mouth is full of sharp teeth
and it has lasers attached to its sides.

Black Manta is a villain who prefers being underwater to life on dry land. He has built a special suit that allows him to breathe underwater. Black Manta wants to lure his enemy, Aquaman, into battle and is using Robin as bait! He knows that both Aquaman and Batman will come to their friend's rescue. The Super Heroes must find Black Manta, retrieve the trident, and save Robin!

The Sea Saucer

This vehicle is designed to glide like a fish. It is capable of extreme speeds and can travel deep underwater.

Red detail stands out in the murky ocean depths

Powerful missiles

Black Manta's face decorates the sub's bow

Weapons systems
- The vehicle is armed with advanced missiles.
- Missile controls are easily accessed from the pilot's seat.

Pipes funnel gas from engine to exhaust

Wide, flat structure provides stability in the water

Rescue Robin!

In an emergency, nothing beats Batman's Batsub for undersea speed! Its sleek design helps Batman zoom through the water. The Batsub's computers find the quickest route to Black Manta's underwater temple lair. Batman and Aquaman race to rescue Robin.

Black Manta is waiting in his submarine, called the Sea Saucer. Aquaman quickly grabs his trident from the top of the temple and breaks Robin's chains. Working together, Batman and Aquaman soon disable the Sea Saucer and defeat Black Manta. Two Super Heroes are better than one!

Green Lantern

Many of Batman's friends fight villains on Earth, but his friend Green Lantern defends the whole universe! He is part of a space police team called the Green Lantern Corps. Green Lantern has a power ring that gives him super-human abilities. He carries a large, green Power Battery to charge the ring.

Green Lantern's power ring allows him to create any object he can imagine. He has used the ring to build an awesome green spaceship, complete with green missiles. His creations are always green in color!

Green Lantern is very powerful, as long as his power ring is charged. His only weakness is that any yellow-colored objects drain his power, even bananas!

Sinestro

Sinestro is an evil alien who used to be a loyal and courageous member of the Green Lantern Corps. He was banished from the team when he began to crave too much power. Now, he is Green Lantern's worst enemy. Sinestro carries yellow weapons that he knows will weaken Green Lantern.

Sinestro has stolen the Power Battery that Green Lantern uses to charge his power ring, and locked it in a bright yellow cage! Green Lantern needs to rescue the Power Battery, but he grows weak when he gets close to the cage. Can Batman help him defeat Sinestro?

Space Batman

Batman has built a special new Space Batsuit, so he can assist Green Lantern in his battle against Sinestro.

Batman's new Space Batsuit is fitted with all the high-tech gadgets Batman needs for his space mission. It has special technology and a mask to allow him to breathe in space. It also has his trusty Utility Belt, with all his best weapons attached. Finally, Batman's Batsuit has special mechanical wings that help him speed through outer space.

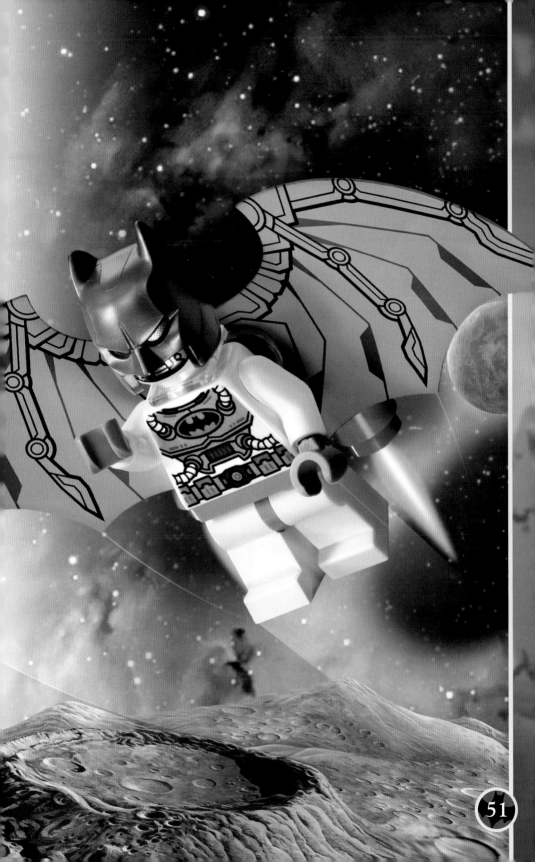

Space Battle

Green Lantern is growing weaker
as his power ring's strength fades.
He cannot go near the yellow cage,
but he fires missiles at Sinestro from
his spaceship while Batman heads
for the imprisoned Power Battery.
Batman breaks into the cage using
a tool from his Utility Belt.

Batman returns the Power Battery to Green Lantern and in an instant his power is fully restored. Together, the heroes defeat Sinestro and lock him in his own yellow cage! Thanks to Batman and Green Lantern, the whole universe is safe once more.

Ready for Anything

Batman is back in Gotham City. He has been very busy helping his fellow Super Heroes battle terrible foes. Together, they have defeated the villains and foiled their evil plans.

For now, Batman is happy to be back at home. He has more Batsuits to design, new vehicles to build, and criminals to watch out for. When evil threatens, Batman is always prepared to leap into action and embark on his next important mission.

R Robin's Blog

Hello! I'm Robin, Batman's friend and trusted sidekick. I interviewed Batman to give my readers an insight into the life of a Super Hero!

Hi Batman! Can I ask you about being Gotham City's greatest hero?

Of course you can Robin, but please be quick. I'm very busy.

What is your favorite thing about being a hero?

I like being able to keep the streets of Gotham City safe.

Previous Posts

- <u>Not so scary now, Scarecrow!</u>
- <u>Seven reasons to wear a cape.</u>
- <u>A sneak peek inside the Batcave.</u>

Really? My favorite thing about being a hero is wearing a cape. It is awesome!

That is true. Our capes are pretty great.

What is the worst thing about being a hero?

I cannot complain. I made a vow to protect the city.

Are you sure there is nothing that annoys you about your job?

Sometimes you annoy me a little. I also don't like it when the Batmobile gets damaged.

I promise that scratch wasn't me! Thanks, Batman.

Quiz

1. Who has Batman taught martial arts to?

2. What is Batgirl's other name?

3. What is James Gordon's job?

4. How do the police call Batman, Robin, and Batgirl?

5. Where is the Joker locked away as punishment for his crimes?

6. Who drives an armored Tumbler car?

7. What does Black Manta steal from Aquaman?

8. What color weakens Green Lantern?

Answers on page 61.

Glossary

Agile
able to move quickly and easily

Alias
a false name or identity

Banished
sent away as punishment for bad behavior

Camouflaged
colored or patterned to blend in to the surrounding area

Commissioner
a senior police officer

Corps
a group of people doing a particular activity

Crave
to want something desperately

Henchman
a sidekick or helper

Lure
to tempt someone with something they want

Martial arts
various sports that can be used in self-defense or attack

Meditation
the practice of clearing or focusing the mind

Scuba
a device that allows the wearer to breathe underwater

Toxic
chemically dangerous or deadly

Trident
a three-pronged spear

Vigilant
aware and observant

Index

Answers to the quiz on pages 58 and 59:
1. Robin 2. Barbara Gordon 3. Gotham City Police
Commissioner 4. They shine the Bat-Signal into the sky
5. Arkham Asylum 6. Bane 7. A golden trident 8. Yellow

Guide for Parents

This book is part of an exciting four-level reading series for children, developing the habit of reading widely for both pleasure and information. These chapter books have a compelling main narrative to suit your child's reading ability. Each book is designed to develop your child's reading skills, fluency, grammar awareness, and comprehension in order to build confidence and engagement when reading.

Ready for a *Level 3* book

YOUR CHILD SHOULD

- be able to read many words without needing to stop and break them down into sound parts.
- read smoothly, in phrases and with expression. By this level, your child will be beginning to read silently.
- self-correct when a word or sentence doesn't sound right.

A VALUABLE AND SHARED READING EXPERIENCE

For some children, text reading, particularly nonfiction, requires much effort, but adult participation can make this both fun and easier. So here are a few tips on how to use this book with your child.

TIP 1 Check out the contents together before your child begins:

- invite your child to check the back cover text, contents page, and layout of the book and comment on it.
- ask your child to make predictions about the story.
- talk about the information your child might want to find out.

TIP 2 Encourage fluent and flexible reading:

- support your child to read in fluent, expressive phrases, making full use of punctuation and thinking about the meaning.

- help your child learn to read with expression by choosing a sentence to read aloud and demonstrating how to do this.

TIP 3 Indicators that your child is reading for meaning:

- your child will be responding to the text if he/she is self-correcting and varying his/her voice.
- your child will want to talk about what he/she is reading or is eager to turn the page to find out what will happen next.

TIP 4 Chat at the end of each chapter:

- encourage your child to recall specific details after each chapter.
- let your child pick out interesting words and discuss what they mean.
- talk about what each of you found most interesting or most important.
- ask questions about the text. These help to develop comprehension skills and awareness of the language used.

A FEW ADDITIONAL TIPS

- Read to your child regularly to demonstrate fluency, phrasing, and expression; to find out or check information; and for sharing enjoyment.
- Encourage your child to reread favorite texts to increase reading confidence and fluency.
- Check that your child is reading a range of different types of material, such as poems, jokes, and following instructions.

Series consultant, **Dr. Linda Gambrell**, Distinguished Professor of Education at Clemson University, has served as President of the National Reading Conference, the College Reading Association, and the International Reading Association.